SKATEBOARDING

TRACE TAYLOR

This is a skateboard.

We love to ride
skateboards.

3

We are girls.

We are boys.

You will see us in the city.

You will see us in the country.

This was made for us.

It's a ramp.

It's a ledge.

So was this.

It's a bowl.

This was made for us...

It's a rail.

...but this wasn't.

It's a pipe.

We love to ride through pipes.

We love to ride through the air.

We jump down
the stairs.

We ride
on walls.

We will ride all day.

We will ride all night.

Many of us can ride on our hands.

All of us will jump to see if we can.

We will all go up on our boards...

...and we will all come down.

Some of us have helmets.

Some of us have helmets and pads.

Some of us have headphones.

Some of us have casts.

25

We're skateboarders.

It's what we love and that's how it is.

POWER WORDS

How many can you read?

1G

a	can	go	it	see	to	what
all	come	have	love	that	up	will
and	down	in	of	the	was	you
are	for	is	on	this	we	
boy	girl	it's	our	through		

2G

but	how	jump	so	wasn't
day	if	many	some	we're